BOOK *of* CAMP FIRE SONGS

ILLUSTRATED *by*

BRIAN DENINGTON

CHRONICLE BOOKS

SAN FRANCISCO

First published in 1995 by
The Appletree Press Ltd
19-21 Alfred Street
Belfast BT2 8DL
Tel: +44 1232 243074
Fax:+44 1232 246756
E-mail: frontdesk@appletree.ie
Web Site: www.irelandseye.com

A Little Book of Campfire Songs

First published in the United States in 1995
by Chronicle Books, 85 Second Street,
San Francisco, CA 94105

Web Site: www.chroniclebooks.com

Distributed in Canada by
Raincoast Books
8680 Cambie Street
Vancouver, B.C. V6P 6M9

ISBN 0-8118-0821-1

9 8 7 6 5 4

Contents

Amazing Grace 4
America (My Country 'tis
   of Thee) 6
Banks of the Ohio 8
Barb'ra Allen 10
Blue Tail Fly 22
Camptown Races 12
Clementine 20
Down in the Valley 18
Goodnight Irene 14
He's Got the Whole World
   in His Hands 16
Home on the Range 24
Juanita 30
Kum Ba Yah 32
Li'l Liza Jane 34
Michael, Row the Boat
   Ashore 36

O Susanna 38
Old Folks at Home 40
Old MacDonald Had a
   Farm 42
On Top of Old Smoky 44
Red River Valley 46
She'll Be Coming Round
   the Mountain 48
Shenandoah 58
Skip to My Lou 50
Someone's in the Kitchen
   with Dinah 52
Taps 60
There's a Hole in My
   Bucket 27
This Land is Your
   Land 54
This Old Man 56

Amazing Grace

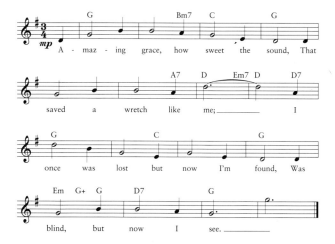

A - maz - ing grace, how sweet the sound, That saved a wretch like me; ____ I once was lost but now I'm found, Was blind, but now I see. ____

'Twas grace that taught my heart to fear,
And grace my fears relieved;
How precious did that grace appear,
The hour I first believed.

Through many dangers, toils and snares,
I have already come.
'Tis grace hath brought me safe thus far,
And grace will lead me home.

How sweet the name of Jesus sounds
In a believer's ear.
It soothes his sorrows, heals his wounds,
And drives away his fear.

Must Jesus bear the cross alone
And all the world go free?
No, there's a cross for everyone
And there's a cross for me.

America (My Country, 'tis of Thee)

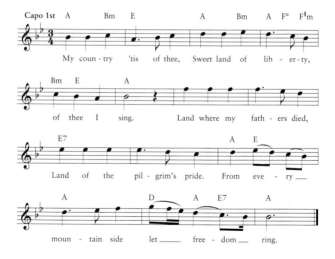

My native country, thee,
Land of the noble free,
Thy name I love,
I love thy rocks and rills,
Thy woods and templed hills;
My heart with rapture thrills
Like that above.

Let music swell the breeze,
And ring from all the trees
Sweet freedom's song;
Let mortal tongues awake,
Let all that breathe partake,
Let rocks their silence break,
The sound prolong.

Our father's God! to thee,
Author of liberty,
To Thee we sing:
Long may our land be bright
With freedom's holy light;
Protect us with Thy might,
Great God, our King.

Banks of the Ohio

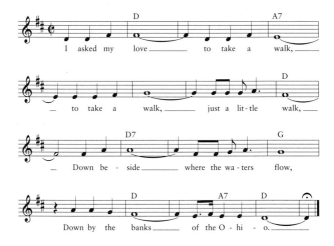

I asked my love _____ to take a walk, _____ _ to take a walk, _____ just a lit-tle walk, _____ _ Down be - side _____ where the wa - ters flow, Down by the banks _____ of the O - hi - o.

Chorus:
And only say that you'll be mine
In no other's arms entwined,
Down beside where the waters flow,
Down by the banks of the Ohio.

I held a knife against her breast
As into my arms she pressed,
She cried, "Oh, Willie, don't murder me,
I'm not prepared for eternity."

Chorus

I started home 'tween twelve and one,
I cried, "My God! what have I done?
Killed the only woman I loved,
Because she would not be my bride."

Chorus

Barb'ra Allen

In Scar - let town, where I was born, There was a fair maid dwel - lin'___ Made ev' - ry youth cry___ "Well - a - day", Her name was Bar - b'ra Al - len. ___

'Twas in the merry month of May
When green buds they were swellin';
Sweet William on his deathbed lay
For love of Barb'ra Allen."

He sent his servant to the town,
The place where she was dwellin'
Cried, "Master bids you come to him,
If your name be Barb'ra Allen."

Well, slowly, slowly got she up
And slowly went she nigh him;
But all she said as she passed his bed,
"Young man, I think you're dying."

She walked out in the green , green fields,
She heard his death bells knellin'.
And every stroke they seemed to say,
"Hard-hearted Barb'ra Allen."

"Oh, father, father, dig my grave,
Go dig it deep and narrow.
Sweet William died for me today;
I'll die for him tomorrow."

They buried her in the old churchyard,
Sweet William's grave was nigh her,
And from his heart grew a red, red rose,
And from her heart a briar.

They grew and grew up the old church wall,
'Till they could grow no higher,
Until they tied a true lover's knot,
The red rose and the briar.

Camptown Races

De Camp-town la-dies sing dis song, Doo-dah! doo-dah! De

Camp-town race track five miles long, Oh! doo-dah day! I

Chorus:

Gwine to run all night! Gwine to run all day! I'll

bet my mo-ney on de bob-tail nag, Some-bod-y bet on de bay.

De long tail filly, and 'de big black hoss,
Doo-dah! doo-dah!
Dey fly de track, an'dey both cut cross,
Oh! doo-dah-day!
De blin hoss sticken in a big mud hole,
Doo-dah! doo-dah!
He can't touch bottom wid a ten-foot pole,
Oh! doo-dah-day!

Chorus

Ol'muley cow come on de track,
Doo-dah! doo-dah!
De bob-tail fling her ober his back,
Oh! doo-dah-day!
Den fly along like a railroad car,
Doo-dah! doo-dah!
A runnin' a race wid a shootin' star,
Oh! doo-dah-day!

Chorus

See dem flyin' on a ten-mile heat,
Doo-dah! doo-dah!
A-roun' de race-track, den repeat,
Oh! doo-dah-day!
I win my money on de bob-tail nag,
Doo-dah! doo-dah!
I keep my money in an old tow-bag,
Oh! doo-dah-day!

Chorus

Goodnight Irene

Chorus:

I - rene, good night; _____ I -

- rene, good night; _____ Good night, I - rene, good

night I - rene, I'll see you in my dreams. _____

Verse:

Last Sat - ur - day night I got mar - ried, _____

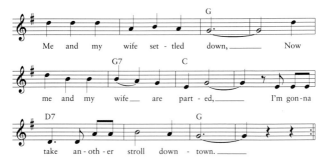

Me and my wife set-tled down, _____ Now
me and my wife _____ are part-ed, _____ I'm gon-na
take an-oth-er stroll down - town. _____

Sometimes I live in the country,
Sometimes I live in town,
Sometimes I take a great notion
To jump into the river and drown.

Chorus

She caused me to weep, she caused me to mourn,
Caused me to leave my home,
But the very last words I heard her say
Was, "Please sing me one more song.'

Chorus

Stop ramblin', stop your gamblin',
Stop stayin' out late at night;
Go home to your wife and your family;
Stay there by your fireside bright.

Chorus

He's Got The Whole World In His Hands

He's got the whole world in His hands, He's got the

whole world in His hands, He's got the whole world

in His hands, He's got the whole world in His hands. ___

He's got the wind and the rain in His hands,
He's got the wind and the rain in His hands,
He's got the wind and the rain in His hands,
He's got the whole world in His hands.

He's got the tiny little baby in His hands,
He's got the tiny little baby in His hands,
He's got the tiny little baby in His hands,
He's got the whole world in His hands.

He's got you and me in His hands,
He's got you and me in His hands,
He's got you and me in His hands,
He's got the whole world in His hands.

Down In The Valley

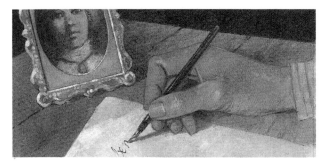

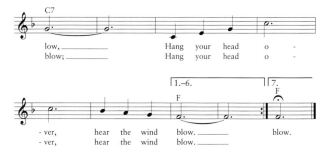

1. Down in the val - ley, val - ley so
Hear the wind blow, love, hear the wind

low, _____ Hang your head o -
blow; _____ Hang your head o -

[1.–6.]   [7.]
- ver, hear the wind blow. _____   blow.
- ver, hear the wind blow. _____

Roses love sunshine, violets love dew;
Angels in Heaven know I love you.
Know I love you, dear, know I love you;
Angels in Heaven know I love you.

If you don't love me, love whom you please;
Throw your arms 'round me, give my heart ease.
Give my heart ease, love, give my heart ease;
Throw your arms 'round me, give my heart ease.

Build me a castle, forty feet high;
So I can see him as he rides by.
As he rides by, love, as he rides by;
So I can see him as he rides by.

Writing this letter, containing three lines,
Answer my question, "Will you be mine?"
Will you be mine, dear, will you be mine?"
Answer my question, "Will you be mine?"

Write me a letter, send it by mail;
Send it in care of Birmingham jail.
Birmingham jail, love, Birmingham jail;
Send it in care of Birmingham jail.

Down in the valley, valley so low,
Hang your head over, hear the wind blow.
Hear the wind blow, love, hear the wind blow;
Hang your head over, hear the wind blow.

Clementine

In a cav - ern in a can - yon, Ex - ca-

-vat - ing for a mine, Dwelt a min - er for - ty-

-nin - er, And his daugh - ter Clem - en - tine.

Chorus:
Oh my darling, oh my darling,
Oh my darling Clementine!
Thou art lost and gone forever,
Dreadful sorry, Clementine.

Light she was and like a fairy,
And her shoes were number nine,
Herring boxes without topses,
Sandals were for Clementine.

Chorus

Drove she ducklings to the water,
Ev'ry morning just at nine,
Hit her foot against a splinter,
Fell into the foaming brine.

Chorus

Ruby lips above the water,
Blowing bubbles soft and fine,
But, alas, I was no swimmer,
So I lost my Clementine.

Chorus

How I missed her! How I missed her,
How I missed my Clementine,
But I kissed her little sister,
I forgot my Clementine.

Chorus

Blue Tail Fly

When I was young I used to wait on my

master and hand him his plate, And pass the bot-tle when

he got dry, And brush a-way the blue tail fly.

Chorus:

Jim-my crack corn and I don't care, Jim-my crack corn and

I don't care, Jim-my crack corn and

I don't care, My mas-ter's gone a - way!_____

And when he'd ride in the afternoon
I'd follow after with a hickory broom;
The pony being rather shy
When bitten by a blue-tail fly.

Chorus

One day he ride around the farm,
The flies so numerous they did swarm;
One chanced to bite him in the thigh;
The devil take the blue-tail fly.

Chorus

The pony run, he jump, he pitch;
He threw my master in the ditch.
He died and the jury wondered why-
The verdict was the blue-tail fly.

Chorus

They lay him under a 'simmon tree;
His epitaph is there to see:
"Beneath this stone I'm forced to lie,
Victim of the blue-tail fly."

Chorus

Home On The Range

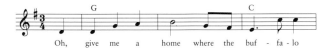

Oh, give me a home where the buf - fa - lo

roam, Where the deer and the an - te - lope play; _____ Where

sel - dom is heard a dis - cour - ag - ing word, And the

skies are not cloud - y all day. _____

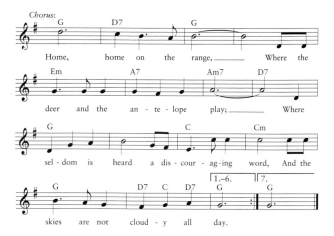

Chorus:

Home, home on the range, _____ Where the deer and the an-te-lope play; _____ Where sel-dom is heard a dis-cour-ag-ing word, And the skies are not cloud-y all day.

Oh, give me a land where the bright diamond sand
Flows leisurely down the stream;
Where the graceful white swan goes gliding along
Like a maid in a heavenly dream.

Chorus

How often at night when the heavens are bright
With the light of the glittering stars,
Have I stood here amazed and asked as I gazed
If their glory exceeds that of ours.

Chorus

Oh, I love these wild flowers in this dear land of ours;
The curfew I love to hear scream;
And I love the white rocks and the antelope flocks
That graze on the mountain-tops green.

Chorus

The red man was pressed from this part of the West,
He's likely no more to return
To the banks of Red River where seldom if ever
Their flickering campfires burn.

Chorus

Where the air is so pure, the zephyrs so free,
The breezes so balmy and light,
That I would not exchange my home on the range
For all the cities so bright.

Chorus

Oh, I would not exchange my home on the range,
Where the deer and the antelope play;
Where seldom is heard a discouraging word
And the skies are not cloudy all day.

Chorus

There's a Hole in My Bucket

There's a hole in my buck-et, dear Li-za, dear Li-za, there's a hole in my buck-et, dear Li-za, a hole!

Then mend it, dear Georgie, dear Georgie, dear Georgie,
Then mend it, dear Georgie, dear Georgie, then mend it!

With what shall I mend it, dear Liza, dear Liza,
With what shall I mend it dear Liza, with what?

With a straw, dear Georgie, dear Georgie, dear Georgie,
With a straw, dear Georgie, dear Georgie, with a straw.

If the straw be too long, dear Liza, dear Liza,
If the straw be too long, dear Liza, too long?

Then cut it, dear Georgie, dear Georgie, dear Georgie,
Then cut it, dear Georgie, dear Georgie, then cut it.

With what shall I cut it, dear Liza, dear Liza,
With what shall I cut it, dear Liza, with what?

With a knife, dear Georgie, dear Georgie, dear Georgie,
With a knife, dear Georgie, dear Georgie, with a knife.

If the knife be too blunt, dear Liza, dear Liza,
If the knife be too blunt, dear Liza, too blunt?

Then sharpen it, dear Georgie, dear Georgie, dear Georgie,
Then sharpen it, dear Georgie, dear Georgie, then sharpen it.

With what shall I sharpen it, dear Liza, dear Liza,
With what shall I sharpen it, dear Liza, with what?

With a stone, dear Georgie, dear Georgie, dear Georgie,
With a stone, dear Georgie, dear Georgie, with a stone.

If the stone be too rough, dear Liza, dear Liza,
If the stone be too rough, dear Liza, too rough?

Then smooth it, dear Georgie, dear Georgie, dear Georgie,
Then smooth it, dear Georgie, dear Georgie, then smooth it.

With what shall I smooth it, dear Liza, dear Liza,
With what shall I smooth it, dear Liza, with what?

With water, dear Georgie, dear Georgie, dear Georgie,
With water, dear Georgie, dear Georgie, with water.

In what shall I fetch it, dear Liza, dear Liza,
In what shall I fetch it, dear Liza, in what?

In a bucket, dear Georgie, dear Georgie, dear Georgie,
In a bucket, dear Georgie, dear Georgie, in a bucket.

(Repeat 1st verse)

Juanita

Capo 1st D7   Bm   G   Gm   A

Soft   o'er the   foun - tain,   Ling -'ring falls the

Em   A7   D7   F♯°   G   Em   A7

south-ern moon;   Far   o'er the   moun -tain,   Breaks the day too

G   D   B°

soon!   In   thy   dark   eyes   splen - dour

Em   A7   D°   D   Bm

Where the warm   light   loves to dwell,   Wea-ry looks,   yet

When in thy dreaming,
Moons like this shall shine again,
And daylight beaming,
Prove thy dreams are vain.
Wilt thou not, relenting,
For thine absent lover sigh,
In thy heart consenting ,
To a pray'r gone by?
Nita Juanita
Let me linger by thy side!
Nita Juanita
Be my own fair bride.

Kum Ba Yah

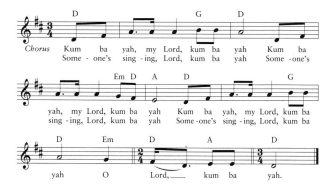

Chorus

Kum ba yah, my Lord, kum ba yah Kum ba yah, my Lord, kum ba yah Kum ba yah, my Lord, kum ba yah O Lord, kum ba yah.

Some - one's sing - ing, Lord, kum ba yah Some - one's sing - ing, Lord, kum ba yah Some - one's sing - ing, Lord, kum ba

Chorus

Someone's laughing, Lord,
Kum ba yah. . . .

Chorus

Someone's crying, Lord
Kum ba yah. . . .

Chorus

Come by here, my Lord,
Kum ba yah. . . .

Chorus

Li'l Liza Jane

I knows a gal that you don't know, L'il Li - za Jane.

Way down south in Bal - ti-mo', Li'l Li - za Jane.

Chorus:

Oh! E - li - za, Li'l Li - za Jane.

Oh! E - li - za, Li'l Li - za Jane.

Liza Jane looks good to me,
Li'l Liza Jane.
Sweetes' one I ever see,
Li'l Liza Jane.

Chorus

I wouldn't care how far we roam,
Li'l Liza Jane,
Where she's at is home, sweet home,
Li'l Liza Jane.

Chorus

Michael, Row The Boat Ashore

Mi - chael row the boat a - shore, Hal - le -

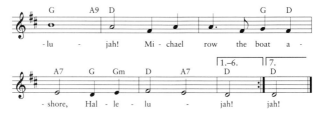

-lu - jah! Mi - chael row the boat a -

- shore, Hal - le - lu - jah! jah!

Brother, lend a helping hand, Hallelujah!
Brother, lend a helping hand, Hallelujah!

Sister, help to trim the sail, Hallelujah!
Sister, help to trim the sail, Hallelujah!

Jordon's River is deep and wide, Hallelujah!
Meet my mother on the other side, Hallelujah!

Jordan's River is chilly cold, Hallelujah!
Kills the body but not the soul, Hallelujah!

Trumpet sound the jubilee, Hallelujah!
Trumpet sound the jubliee, Hallelujah!

Michael, row the boat ashore, Hallelujah!
Michael, row the boat ashore, Hallelujah!

Oh, Susanna!

I— come from Al - a - ba - ma with my ban - jo on my knee, I'm— going to Louis - i - a - na, My Su - san - na for to see.

Chorus:

Oh, Su - sa - na! Oh, don't you cry for me, For I come from A - la - ba - ma with my ban - jo on my knee.

It rained all day the night I left
The weather was so dry,
The sun so hot I froze myself,
Susanna, don't you cry.

Chorus

I had a dream the other night,
When everything was still.
I thought I saw Susanna
A-coming down the hill.

Chorus

The buckwheat cake was in her mouth,
The tear was in her eye,
Says I, "I'm coming from the South."
Susanna, don't you cry.

Chorus

Old Folks At Home

Way down up-on the Swa-nee Riv-er, Far, far a-

- way, There's where my heart is turn-ing ev-er,

There's where the old folks stay. All up and down the

whole cre-a-tion, Sad-ly I roam, Still long-ing for the

old plan - ta - tion, And for the old folks at home. All the world is
sad and drear - y Ev - 'ry where I roam, Oh, how __ my __
heart grows wear - y, Far from the old folks at home.

All 'round the little farm I wandered
When I was young,
Then many happy days I squandered,
Many the songs I sung.
When I was playing with my brother
Happy was I.
Oh! take me to my kind old mother,
There let me live and die.

Chorus

One little hut among the bushes,
One that I love,
Still sadly to my mem'ry rushes,
No matter where I rove.
When will I see the bees a-humming
All 'round the comb?
When will I hear the banjo strumming
Down in my good old home?

Chorus

Old MacDonald Had A Farm

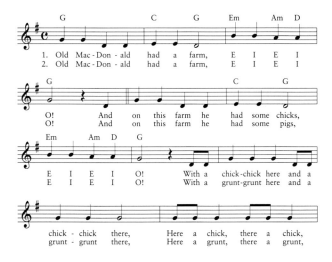

1. Old Mac-Don-ald had a farm, E I E I O! And on this farm he had some chicks, E I E I O! With a chick-chick here and a chick - chick there, Here a chick, there a chick,

2. Old Mac-Don-ald had a farm, E I E I O! And on this farm he had some pigs, E I E I O! With a grunt-grunt here and a grunt - grunt there, Here a grunt, there a grunt,

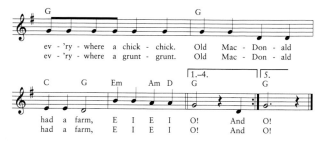

ev - 'ry - where a chick - chick. Old Mac - Don - ald
ev - 'ry - where a grunt - grunt. Old Mac - Don - ald

had a farm, E I E I O! And O!
had a farm, E I E I O! And O!

Old Mac-Donald had a farm
E I E I O
And on this farm he had some turkeys (gobble, gobble),
E I E I O!
With a gobble-gobble here and a gobble-gobble there,
Here a gobble, there a gobble,
ev'ry-where a gobble-gobble.
Old Mac-Donald had a farm,
E I E I O!
And on this farm he had some sheep (baa, baa),
E I E I O!
With a baa-baa here and a baa-baa there,
Here a baa, there a baa,
ev'ry-where a baa-baa.
Old Mac-Donald had a farm,
E I E I O!
And on this farm he had some cows (moo, moo),
E I E I O!
With a moo-moo here and a moo-moo there,
Here a moo, there a moo,
ev'ry-where a moo-moo.
Old Mac-Donald had a farm,
E I E I O!

On Top of Old Smoky

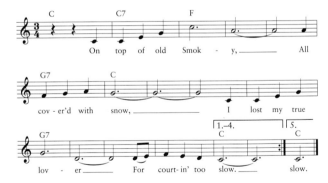

On top of old Smok - y, _____ All cov - er'd with snow, _____ I lost my true lov - er _____ For court- in' too slow. _____ slow.

Now courtin's a pleasure
But partin' is grief,
A false hearted lover
Is worse than a thief.

A thief will just rob you
And take what you have,
But a false hearted lover
Will send you to your grave.

They'll hug you and kiss you
And tell you more lies,
Than cross-ties on the railroad
Or stars in the skies.

On top of Old Smoky,
All covered with snow,
I lost my true lover
For courtin' too slow.

Red River Valley

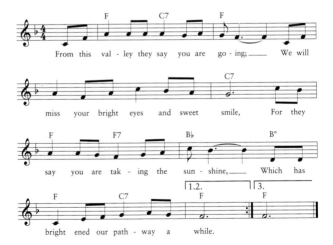

From this val - ley they say you are go - ing; ____ We will miss your bright eyes and sweet smile, For they say you are tak - ing the sun - shine, ____ Which has bright ened our path - way a while.

Chorus:
Come and sit by my side if you love me,
Do not hasten to bid me adieu,
But remember the Red River Valley
And the girl that has loved you so true.

Won't you think of the valley you're leaving?
Oh how lonely, how sad it will be,
Oh think of the fond heart you're breaking,
And the grief you are causing me.

Chorus

I have promised you, my darling, that never
Will a word from my lips cause you pain;
And my life, it will be yours forever
If you only will love me again.

Chorus

She'll be Comin' Round the Mountain

She'll be com-in' round the moun-tain when she comes,

She'll be com-in' round the moun-tain when she comes,

She'll be com-in' round the moun-tain, She'll be com-in' round the

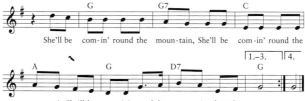

moun- tain She'll be com- in' round the moun-tain when she comes.

She'll be driv'in six white horses when she comes,
She'll be driv'in six white horses when she comes,
She'll be driv'in six white horses
She'll be driv'in six white horses
She'll be driv'in six white horses when she comes.

Oh, we'll all go to meet her when she comes,
Oh, we'll all go to meet her when she comes,
Oh, we'll all go to meet her,
Oh, we'll all go to meet her,
Oh, we'll all go to meet her when she comes.

We'll be singin' "Hallelujah" when she comes,
We'll be singin' "Hallelujah" when she comes,
We'll be singin' "Hallelujah,"
We'll be singin' "Hallelujah,"
We'll be singin' "Hallelujah" when she comes

Skip to My Lou

Lost my part-ner what-'ll I do? Lost my part-ner what-'ll I do?

Lost my part-ner what-'ll I do? Skip to my Lou, my dar-lin'.

Chorus:

Lou, Lou, skip to my Lou, Lou, Lou skip to my Lou,

Lou, Lou, skip to my Lou, Skip to my Lou, my dar-lin'.

I'll get another one, purtier'n you,
I'll get another one, purtier'n you,
I'll get another one, purtier'n you,
Skip to my Lou, My darlin' . . .

Chorus

Can't get a red bird, a blue bird'll do,
Can't get a red bird, a blue bird'll do,
Can't get a red bird, a blue bird'll do,
Skip to my Lou, my darlin' . . .

Chorus

Little red wagon, painted blue.

Chorus

Fly in the sugar-bowl, shoo, fly, shoo.

Chorus

Gone again, what'll I do?

Chorus

Hair in the butterdish, six feet long.

Chorus

Cows in the cornfield, two by two.

Chorus

Rats in the breadtray, how they chew.

Chorus

One old boot and a run-down shoe.

Chorus

Someone's in the Kitchen with Dinah

I've been work-ing on the rail - road all the live long day. ___ I've been work-ing on the rail - road Just to pass the time a - way. ___ Can't you hear the whis-tle blow - ing, rise up ear - ly in the morn? ___ Can't you

This Land Is Your Land

Chorus:

This land is your land, this land is my land, __

__ From Cal - i - for - nia _____ to the New York

Is - land, __ From the red-wood for - est _____ to the Gulf Stream

wa - ter, _____ This land was made for you and

me. _____ As I went walk-ing _____ that rib-bon of high-way, _____ I saw a-bove me _____ that end-less sky-way, _____ I saw be-low me _____ that gol-den val-ley, _____ This land was made for you and me. _____ This land is me _____ This land was made for you and me.

I roamed and I rambled and I followed my footsteps
To the sparkling sands of her diamond deserts,
While all around me a voice was sounding,
Saying "This land was made for you and me."

Chorus

The sun came shining and I was strolling,
And the wheat fields waving and the dust clouds rolling,
As the fog was lifting, a voice was chanting,
"This land was made for you and me."

Chorus

This Old Man

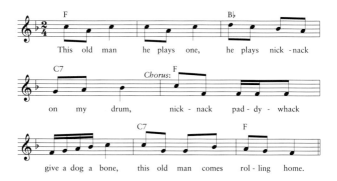

This old man he plays one, he plays nick-nack

on my drum, nick-nack pad-dy-whack

give a dog a bone, this old man comes rol-ling home.

This old man he plays two,
He plays nicknack on my shoe,

Chorus

This old man he plays three,
He plays nicknack on my tree,

Chorus

This old man he plays four,
He plays nicknack on my door,

Chorus

This old man he plays five,
He plays nicknack on my hive,

Chorus

This old man he plays six,
He plays nicknack on my sticks,

Chorus

This old man he plays seven,
He plays nicknack up in heaven,

Chorus

This old man he plays eight,
He plays nicknack on my gate,

Chorus

This old man he plays nine,
He plays nicknack on my vine,

Chorus

This old man he plays ten,
He plays nicknack over again.

Chorus

Shenandoah

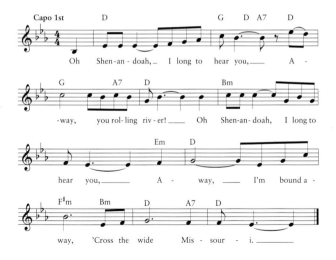

Oh Shen-an-doah, I long to hear you, A-way, you rol-ling riv-er! Oh Shen-an-doah, I long to hear you, A - way, I'm bound a-way, 'Cross the wide Mis - sour - i.

The white man loved an Indian maiden,
Away, you rolling river!
With notions his canoe was laden,
Away, I'm bound away,
'Cross the wide Missouri.

Oh, Shenandoah, I love your daughter,
Away, you rolling river!
For her I've crossed the stormy water,
Away, I'm bound away,
'Cross the wide Missouri.

Farewell, my dear, I'm bound to leave you,
Away, you rolling river!
Oh, Shenandoah, I'll not deceive you,
Away, I'm bound away!
'Cross the wide Missouri.

Taps

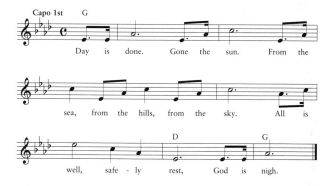

Day is done. Gone the sun. From the sea, from the hills, from the sky. All is well, safe - ly rest, God is nigh.